# Flavou

# SUR

## RECIPES

Compiled by Julia Skinner

# THE FRANCIS FRITH COLLECTION

www.francisfrith.com

First published in the United Kingdom in 2013 by The Francis Frith Collection®

This edition published exclusively for Bradwell Books in 2013
For trade enquiries see: www.bradwellbooks.com or tel: 0800 834 920
ISBN 978-1-84589-741-3

British Library Cataloguing in Publication Data

Flavours of Surrey - Recipes
Compiled by Julia Skinner

The Francis Frith Collection
6 Oakley Business Park,
Wylye Road, Dinton,
Wiltshire SP3 5EU
Tel: +44 (0) 1722 716 376
Email: info@francisfrith.co.uk

**www.francisfrith.com**

Printed and bound in Malaysia
Contains material sourced from responsibly managed forests

Front Cover: **COBHAM, THE TREE HOUSE AT THE OLD OAK TREE RESTAURANT
1911** 63123xp
Frontispiece: **REIGATE, HIGH STREET 1919** 68894
Contents: **MILFORD, FARMING c1955** M76060

*The colour-tinting is for illustrative purposes only, and is not intended to be historically accurate*

# CONTENTS

Since the mid 19th century watercress has been grown around Abinger Hammer in the Tillingbourne valley near Dorking, where a local landmark is the large clock that overhangs the A25, featuring a figure of Jack the Smith that strikes the bell every hour. In the late 19th and early 20th centuries a huge quantity of the leafy green crop was grown each year, most of which was sent by train from Gomshall station to supply the London wholesale markets. Although production is now only a fraction of what it once was, watercress is still grown by R Coe and Sons in Abinger Hammer and is available from the Kingfisher Farm Shop in the village (see: www. kingfisherfarmshop.com). It is grown in natural, mineral-rich spring water of the highest purity, which provides all the necessary nutrients the crop needs without the aid of fertilisers or pesticides.

**ABINGER HAMMER
THE CLOCK
1909** 61362

# RECIPE

## WATERCRESS SOUP

Watercress is a super-food packed with nutrients, with a distinctive peppery, slightly bitter, flavour. It can be eaten raw as a salad or in sandwiches, used in cooking, for instance as a filling in a savoury flan (as in the recipe on page 4), or to make a sauce to accompany fish such as trout or salmon, but is best known for making a delicious soup. Serves 4-6.

2-3 bunches or bags of watercress
(approximately 200g/7oz total weight)
25g/1oz butter
1 medium sized onion, peeled and chopped
225g/8oz potatoes, peeled and chopped
1.2 litres/2 pints chicken or vegetable stock
Salt and freshly ground black pepper
Freshly grated nutmeg, to serve (optional)
125ml/4 fl oz single cream, crème fraîche or natural yogurt,
to serve (optional)

Melt the butter in a large saucepan. Add the chopped onion and cook over a medium heat for 4-5 minutes, until soft and transparent but not browned. Add the chopped potatoes and cook for a further 4-5 minutes, stirring occasionally to prevent sticking, then add the stock. Chop through the bunches of watercress about one third from the leafy ends, and retain the leafy section for later. Roughly chop the stalks and any remaining leaves on them, and add to the pan – the stalks help flavour the soup. Bring the soup to the boil, then reduce the heat, cover the pan and simmer gently for about 20 minutes, until the potato pieces are soft and tender. Stir in the reserved watercress and allow to heat through for about 3 minutes. Remove the pan from the heat and allow the soup to cool for a few minutes, then liquidise with a blender or food processor. Return the soup to the rinsed out pan, reheat and season to taste with salt and freshly ground black pepper, and a little freshly grated nutmeg, if using. Serve, adding a swirl of single cream, crème fraîche or natural yogurt to each helping if liked.

# RECIPE

## SMOKED TROUT AND WATERCRESS FLAN

Abinger Hammer near Dorking is also the home of the Tillingbourne Trout Farm, on Dorking Road (website: tillingbournetrout.com). They have their own smokery on the premises, and as well as selling fresh trout straight from the water their farm shop also sells an extensive range of hot and cold smoked fish, including whole smoked trout and trout fillets. Smoked trout and watercress are used to make this savoury tart that can be eaten warm or cold. It makes an ideal dish for a summer lunch or picnic. If you can't get smoked trout you can use salmon fillet instead, poached, then cooled and flaked.

| For the pastry: | For the filling: |
|---|---|
| 225g/8oz plain flour | 15g/ ½ oz butter |
| 100g/4oz butter or margarine | 4 spring onions |
| Pinch of salt | 1 bunch or bag of watercress (about 100g/4oz in weight) |
| | 150ml/5 fl oz double cream |
| | 150ml/5fl oz crème fraîche |
| | 2 medium eggs |
| | 100g/4oz smoked trout fillets, roughly flaked |

Grease a tart or flan tin or dish about 25cms (10ins) in diameter and make the pastry: put the flour into a mixing bowl with a pinch of salt, and rub in the butter or margarine until the mixture resembles fine breadcrumbs. Add 2-3 tablespoonfuls of cold water, just enough to mix it together to form a firm dough, then knead the dough lightly until it is smooth and elastic. Roll out the pastry dough on a lightly floured surface and use it to line the flan tin or dish. Put the lined pastry case in the fridge to chill for 15 minutes. Whilst it is chilling, pre-heat the oven to 200ºC/400ºF/Gas Mark 6.

Prick the chilled pastry base all over with a fork, to allow air bubbles to escape during cooking. Line the pastry case with a piece of greaseproof or baking paper, and fill it with baking beans or alternative, such as dry uncooked rice. Place in the centre of the pre-heated oven and bake blind for 10 minutes. Remove from the oven and take out the greaseproof paper

and baking beans, then return to the oven for a further 8-10 minutes, until the pastry is dry and has turned a light golden brown. Remove from the oven, and reduce the oven temperature to 180°C/350°C/Gas Mark 4.

Trim the spring onions, keeping as much of the green part as possible, and chop into small pieces. Melt the 25g (1oz) butter in a large pan, add the spring onions and sauté gently for a few minutes until they are soft. Chop off the coarse stalks from the watercress and roughly chop the rest. Add to the pan, and cook gently for about a minute until it just starts to wilt, then remove the pan from the heat and set aside.

Beat together the eggs, cream and crème fraîche and season well. Spread the spring onion and watercress over the base of the cooked pastry case, then add the flaked smoked trout and mix it all about a bit. Pour over the egg and cream mixture. Bake in the oven at the reduced temperature for about 30 minutes, until the filling is golden and just set. Allow the flan to settle and cool before serving warm, or otherwise serve cold.

**WEYBRIDGE, THE VIEW FROM THE LINCOLN ARMS HOTEL**
**1890** 23589

# RECIPE

## BAKED TROUT WITH HERB STUFFING

This old recipe for trout baked in the oven originally called for 'savoury herbs' in the stuffing. This term covered all the common garden herbs, so although parsley, thyme and rosemary are specified here, you could equally well substitute marjoram, dill, tarragon, fennel, lovage or chervil. Serves 4.

> 4 medium-sized trout, each weighing about 255g/10oz,
>    gutted and cleaned (with the heads left on)
> 100g/4oz fresh soft breadcrumbs, white or wholemeal as preferred
> 2 tablespoonfuls finely chopped mixed fresh herbs – parsley,
>    lemon thyme and rosemary (or other herbs of choice)
> Finely grated zest and juice of half a lemon
> Salt and freshly ground black pepper
> Pinch of freshly ground nutmeg
> 1 egg, beaten
> 25g/1oz butter, cut into small pieces
> 50ml/2fl oz (2 tablespoonfuls) dry white wine

Pre-heat the oven to 180°C/350°F/Gas Mark 4 and liberally butter a wide, shallow ovenproof dish large enough to hold the 4 trout laid head to tail in one layer.

Mix the breadcrumbs, herbs, lemon zest and nutmeg in a bowl, and season to taste with salt and freshly ground black pepper. Add the beaten egg and mix together well to form the stuffing mixture and use it to fill the cavity of each fish. Secure the edges of the cavities together with skewers or wooden cocktails sticks, or parcel up each fish with kitchen string. Arrange the stuffed fish in the buttered dish and dot the top of each fish with small pieces of butter. Pour in the wine and lemon juice. Cover the dish with its lid or a tightly-fitted piece of kitchen foil and bake in the pre-heated oven for about 30 minutes, until the fish are tender. Remove the sticks or string and serve the trout with some of the buttery cooking liquid from the pan spooned over each fish.

# RECIPE

## WATER SOUCHY

Water souchy is a very simple fish stew. It originates from Holland where it is a very popular dish – its name comes from the Dutch 'waterzootje' – and it was introduced into England from that country in the late 17th century, during the reign of Queen Mary II and her husband and joint monarch, King William III, Prince of the Dutch state of Orange.

Water souchy is usually made with a variety of freshwater fish, but the Surrey town of Dorking was famous in the past for a particular version that was made there, using locally caught perch and tench from the streams in the neighbourhood and flounders brought up from Brighton on the Sussex coast. It was so popular that Dutch merchants based in London came frequently to the town to sample the local delicacy. The 'Gentlemen's Dorking Club' used to meet every other Thursday from June to November to enjoy water souchy at the Red Lion, whilst the Dutch merchants were particularly partial to the version served at the King's Head. The recipe was recorded in an old issue of the Surrey Archaeological Collections (the journal of the Archaeological Society), taken from an 1833 cookery book 'by a Lady', and is given here in its original form for interest's sake:

'Stew two or three flounders, some parsley roots and leaves, thirty peppercorns, and a quart of water, till the fish are boiled to pieces; pulp them through a sieve. Set over the fire the pulped fish, the liquor that boiled them, some perch, tench or flounders, and some fresh roots or leaves of parsley; simmer all till done enough, then serve in a deep dish. Slice of bread and butter are to be sent to table to eat with the souchy.'

*(As quoted in: 'Highways and Byways in Surrey', Eric Parker, 1908, Macmillan & Co, London)*

Surrey used to be a considerably larger county than it is now, with the River Thames forming much of its northern boundary. The 1889 London Government Act that created the new county of London captured part of Surrey and annexed the south bank of the Thames – the bank still lovingly referred to by those who ply the river as 'the Surrey side'. Further incursions took place in 1965 and again in 1974, when the old county of Middlesex was abolished, so that Staines, on the north bank of the Thames, became a Surrey town. Today, Surrey has lost much of its traditional northern boundary along the Thames, but it still lays claim to sufficient of England's 'Royal River' through Staines and Chertsey, Walton-on-Thames and Weybridge, for this old watery highway to be an integral part of the county.

**WALTON-ON-THAMES, THE SWAN HOTEL 1908** 60037

# RECIPE

## Eel Pie

The River Thames used to be full of sweet-tasting eels. Migrating elvers, or young eels, once wriggled their way up the Thames in such multitudes that in 1902 one author wrote that 'they made a black margin to the river, on either side of the banks'. Eel Pie was a very popular dish in the past, and gave its name to Eel Pie Island in the Thames at Richmond-upon-Thames, which was in Surrey until the formation of the London Borough of Richmond-upon-Thames in 1965 made it part of Greater London. In the 19th century the island was a popular resort for steamer excursions along the Thames from London and was famous for the eel pies served there, which gave it its nickname. Eels are not so common in the Thames now, but are often caught by anglers on the River Wey.

> 1.4kg/3 lbs skinned eels
> 300ml/ ½ pint fish stock
> Salt and pepper
> 1 bunch of fresh herbs
> 1 tablespoonful finely chopped fresh parsley
> 100g/4oz onions, peeled and thinly sliced
> 1 tablespoonful lemon juice
> 225g/8oz shortcrust or puff pastry, as preferred
> 1 egg

Wash the eels, cut them into small pieces and place them in a pan. Add the fish stock, salt and pepper, the bunch of herbs and onions, and simmer gently until the eel pieces are tender enough for the bones to be removed. Arrange the boned eels in a pie dish, and add the chopped parsley, lemon juice and enough strained stock to cover the eels (reserve the rest in case needed – see below). Cover with a lid of pastry, brush with beaten egg and bake in a hot oven for about 45 minutes (225°C/425°F/Gas Mark 6). A little extra stock may be poured into the pie through a hole in the centre of the pastry before serving.

# RECIPE

### CHEESE PUDDINGS

This recipe for individual savoury cheese puddings was collected in Surrey and included by May Byron in her cookery book 'Pot Luck' of 1914. She titled them 'Egg and Cheese Ramekins' and noted at the end of the recipe that 'these never fail to please'. They make an ideal snack or supper dish to serve with bread and butter or perhaps a salad. Serves 4.

> 2 large eggs (size matters!)
> 50g/2oz Cheddar cheese, grated
> 2 tablespoonfuls whole (full fat) milk or single cream
> 1 teaspoonful plain flour, mixed to a smooth paste with
>    1 teaspoonful of milk
> Freshly ground black pepper
> 50g/2oz butter

Pre-heat the oven to 200°C/400°F/Gas Mark 6 and butter four small ramekin pots.

Melt the butter in a pan over a gentle heat, then leave to cool a little. Beat the eggs in a bowl with the milk or cream, then stir in the flour and milk mixture and grated cheese. Season to taste with freshly ground pepper, but salt should not be necessary as the cheese already makes the mixture salty. Pour in the melted butter and mix it all together well. Divide the mixture between the ramekin pots – it should only fill them about halfway up. Stand the pots on a baking tray or similar and bake just below the centre of the pre-heated oven for 15-20 minutes, until they are risen and golden brown, and firm to the touch.

**HOLCOMBE, GIRLS IN MARE LANE 1908** 61127x

# RECIPE

### NORBURY BLUE CHEESE AND BROCCOLI FLAN

Surrey's only cheesemaker is the Norbury Blue Cheese Company, based near Mickleham at the foot of Box Hill. All their cheese is made solely from milk produced by the cows on Norbury Park Farm where the company is based. Their flagship cheese is Norbury Blue, a terrific blue cheese made from unpasteurised milk; its distinct flavour earned it a rating as one of Britain's Best Cheeseboard Choices in the Restaurant Magazine in March 2011. Norbury Blue is supplied to farm shops around the county, from Garsons in Esher to Priory Farm near Redhill as well as delis and good food shops throughout Surrey – it is not available in supermarkets. It can also be bought online from the company's website – www.norburyblue.co.uk – where you can find details of stockists. This recipe uses Norbury Blue to make a savoury flan to serve either warm or cold for summer lunches, or taken on a picnic to eat cold. If you can't get Norbury Blue, try making this with an alternative blue cheese like Stilton, Blue Shropshire or St Agur.

>       225g/8oz plain flour
>       100g/4oz butter or margarine
>       225g/8oz trimmed weight of broccoli florets
>       175g/6oz Norbury Blue cheese (or alternative)
>       3 eggs
>       300ml/ ½ pint single cream
>       Salt and freshly ground black pepper

Grease a flan tin or dish about 25cms (10 inches) in diameter. Put the flour in a mixing bowl with a pinch of salt, and rub in the butter or margarine. Add 2-3 tablespoonfuls of cold water, just enough to mix it together to form a firm dough, then knead the dough lightly until smooth. Roll out the dough and use it to line the flan tin.
Put the lined pastry case in the fridge to chill for 15 minutes.

Whilst it is chilling, pre-heat the oven to 200ºC/400ºF/Gas Mark 6.

Prick the chilled pastry base all over with a fork, to allow air bubbles to escape during cooking. Line the pastry case with a piece of greaseproof or baking paper, and fill it with baking beans or alternative, such as dry uncooked rice. Place in the centre of the pre-heated oven and bake blind for 10 minutes. Take out the greaseproof paper and baking beans, then return to the oven for a further 8-10 minutes, until the pastry is dry and a light golden brown. Remove from the oven, and reduce the oven temperature to 180°C/350°F/Gas Mark 4.

While the pastry case is cooking, prepare the broccoli florets. Bring a pan of water to the boil, and add the trimmed florets. Bring the water back to a brisk boil, cook the broccoli for 2 minutes, then remove from the heat and drain the broccoli thoroughly. Arrange the broccoli florets in the pastry case. Cut the cheese into small pieces and scatter them over and around the broccoli florets.

Beat together the eggs and cream, and season to taste with salt and pepper. Pour the mixture into the pastry case over the broccoli and cheese. Bake at the reduced temperature for 30-40 minutes, until the flan is cooked but not dry and the filling is risen and just firm to the touch.

This should not be eaten hot, straight from the oven, but leave it to cool a little and eat it warm, or otherwise leave it to cool completely before eating.

Delivery vans are seen here parked outside Caterham's Railway Hotel, which was built in 1856 when the railway arrived in the town; the hotel was demolished in 1902, to be replaced by Grand Parade. The coming of the railway to Surrey in the 19th century was of great importance to the county, stimulating the development of new 'railway towns' such as Redhill, Woking and Surbiton, as well as the growth of older centres along the routes of the railway lines. The railways not only brought more people to live in the county but also allowed fresh produce to be transported quickly into the capital, widening the market for perishable goods. This stimulated an important market gardening industry in Surrey, especially in the north-east of the county.

**CATERHAM, THE RAILWAY HOTEL 1894** 34290

# RECIPE

## Spring Vegetables in Sauce

This can be served as a vegetarian main course garnished with croutons, or as a vegetable dish to accompany meat or fish. It is an unusual way of cooking very small, tender young vegetables that only require a short cooking time.

50g/2oz butter
8 small young carrots, scraped
16 small new potatoes, scraped
16 spring onions, peeled and trimmed
Bouquet garni of thyme, parsley and mint sprigs
    tied together with kitchen string
1 tablespoonful plain flour
300ml/ ½ pint vegetable or chicken stock
150ml/ ¼ pint dry white wine
225g/8oz shelled peas, fresh or frozen
225g/8oz shelled broad beans, fresh or frozen
1 teaspoonful salt
1 teaspoonful caster sugar
1 tablespoonful double cream

Melt the butter in a saucepan, add the carrots, potatoes and spring onions, and toss well to coat. Add the herbs. Sprinkle in the flour, then gradually stir in the stock and wine. Cover and simmer for 10 minutes. Stir in the peas and broad beans and simmer for a further 10 minutes until all the vegetables are tender. Remove from the heat and stir in the salt, sugar and cream. Transfer to a heated serving dish and serve.

### 'KING WILLIAM ALWAYS ATE THE STALKS.'

The 17th century was a great age of improved vegetables in England, when gardeners looked particularly to Holland for better varieties and new kinds to cultivate. In the 1680s and 90s Moor Park near Farnham was the home of the statesman and diplomat Sir William Temple (1628-1699). Sir William was a keen gardener as well as a writer on the subject and created a famous garden there, where a regular visitor was King William III, the Dutch husband of Queen Mary II who ruled with her as joint monarch. At that time, Sir William's secretary was a young man called Jonathan Swift (1667-1745), later to be famous as the author of 'Gulliver's Travels'. He recorded how on one visit to Moor Park King William showed him the Dutch method of cutting the new, improved strain of asparagus from Holland which Sir William was growing in the garden there, showing him how to cut it with a short rather than a wide stroke of the knife, so the smaller stalks remained undamaged for later cutting. King William also explained how this type of asparagus was so tender it could all be eaten, including the stalks. Jonathan Swift recalled this later in life when, as Dean Swift, he had his own household – he is said to have refused to allow a guest a second helping of asparagus until he had cleared the stalks on his plate, telling him that 'King William always ate the stalks'.

British asparagus is probably the best in the world, as our climate allows the stems to develop slowly, producing a full, sweet flavour and a fine tender texture, but its season is very short – about six weeks, from early May until about the end of June. It should also be eaten as soon as possible after picking, for the best flavour. Several farm shops in Surrey sell locally grown asparagus, and in some places you can pick-your-own, including Garsons Farm at Esher, Crockford Bridge at Weybridge and Secretts at Milford – you won't get better, tastier asparagus than that!

# RECIPE

### ASPARAGUS IN HOLLANDAISE SAUCE

Asparagus is best cooked very simply: cut or break off the woody ends of the stalks then use a sharp knife or vegetable peeler to scrape off any fibrous scales, starting about 5cms (2 inches) down from the tips. Either tie the trimmed spears into a bundle with string and stand them upright in a narrow, deep pan with boiling salted water to come halfway up the stems, cover the pan with a lid or piece of foil, and steam for 10-20 minutes, depending on their thickness, or add the asparagus to a pan of gently simmering, salted water and cook until tender, allowing 2-3 minutes for thin spears and 5-8 minutes for finger-thick spears, then drain well; alternatively, brush the spears with a little olive oil and keep turning them under a hot grill for a few minutes until tender. Serve with melted butter and perhaps a squeeze of lemon juice and a little salt and pepper. However, you might like to recall the connection with Moor Park, asparagus and the Dutch King William III by serving asparagus with Hollandaise Sauce. Serves 4 as a starter.

> 2 bunches of asparagus (about 500g/1lb 2oz),
>    prepared and cooked as above
> 2 tablespoonfuls white wine vinegar
> 2 egg yolks
> 100g/4oz butter
> Juice of half a lemon
> Salt and freshly ground black pepper

Melt the butter in a pan, then leave to cool a little. In another pan, bring the vinegar to the boil and let it bubble until it has reduced by half to just 1 tablespoonful. Remove from the heat and add 1 tablespoonful cold water. Whisk the egg yolks into the vinegar and water mixture, then put the pan over a very low heat and whisk until the mixture just starts to thicken. Remove the pan from the heat and continue whisking until the sauce thickens completely, as it will continue to cook in the pan. Gradually whisk in the melted butter to form a thick, smooth sauce. Whisk in the lemon juice and add seasoning to taste. Serve immediately with the drained asparagus.

**CHERTSEY, GUILDFORD STREET 1908** 60929

Until the mid 20th century the growing of hops for the brewing industry was a big part of Farnham's economy, and huge areas of farmland around the town were devoted to their cultivation. Today, just one hop garden in the area remains, at the Hampton Estate near Puttenham, between Farnham and Guildford, which supplies old-fashioned Fuggles hops to the award-winning Hogs Back

Brewery at nearby Tongham, Surrey's largest independent brewery (www.hogsback.co.uk). Famous for its flagship TEA (Traditional English Ale), the brewery's other products include Hop Garden Gold, Hogs Back Bitter, England's Glory, Gardeners Tipple and RIP Snorter.

**FARNHAM, THE BOROUGH 1913** 65926

# RECIPE

## BEEF BRAISED IN HOG'S BACK BEER

Use a Hogs Back Brewery beer of your choice to make this beef stew with a rich gravy. Beer used in cooking should be of room heat, not chilled, and slightly flat, so open the bottle and decant it into a glass or jug a few minutes before using it in this recipe. If you can't get a Hogs Back brew, use your own favourite beer instead. Serves 4-6.

900g/2 lbs lean braising or stewing steak, cut into cubes
500ml/18fl oz (1 bottle) Hogs Back Brewery beer of choice
1-2 tablespoonfuls cooking oil
3 medium-sized onions, peeled and cut into quarters
2 garlic cloves, crushed
1 rounded tablespoonful plain flour
1 teaspoonful dried mixed herbs
2 bay leaves
Salt and freshly ground black pepper

Pre-heat the oven to 150°C/300°F/Gas Mark 2. Heat one tablespoonful of the oil in a very large frying pan and fry the cubes of meat in small batches, a few pieces at a time, until they are well browned on all sides. As you brown the meat, remove it to a plate. When all the meat has been browned, add a little more oil to the pan if necessary, put in the sliced onions and fry for about five minutes until they are lightly browned at the edges, stirring them around as they cook. After that add the crushed garlic, let that cook for about 30 seconds, then turn the heat down, return the meat to the pan and sprinkle over the flour. Stir around with a wooden spoon until all the flour has been absorbed into the pan juices. Gradually stir in the beer, a little at a time, then turn up the heat and bring it to simmering point, stirring continually, until the sauce has thickened and is starting to bubble. Add the mixed herbs, bay leaves and salt and pepper. Pour it into a large casserole dish, cover with its lid and cook in the centre of the pre-heated oven for a full 2½ hours for the beer to mellow and become a tasty sauce. Serve with boiled, mashed or baked potatoes and seasonal vegetables.

The Downs around Epsom and Banstead have long been famous for the splendid sheep raised there, producing a well-flavoured meat redolent of the herbs they grazed upon on the short, sweet turf. Epsom is also famous as the venue for the two great classic flat horse-races run on the Epson Downs Racecourse south of the town, the Derby and the Oaks, but it has a place in Britain's food history as the home in the 1840s and 50s of Isabella Mayson, whose stepfather was the clerk of the racecourse. Isabella lived at Ormonde House at the east end of Epsom's High Street, which was replaced by a shopping parade in the 1890s. In 1856 Isabella Mayson married Samuel Beeton at St Martin's Church in Epsom, and went on to achieve huge celebrity as the Victorian food guru Mrs Beeton, author of the famous 'Book of Household Management'.

**EPSOM, HIGH STREET 1907** 58595

# RECIPE

## SURREY LAMB PIE

The traditional Surrey version of this pie was made with mutton chops and topped with just the layer of sliced mushrooms, but a pastry lid is given here to make a more substantial meal. Puff pastry can be used instead of shortcrust, if preferred.

> 8 small lamb chops or cutlets, trimmed of excess fat
> 25g/1oz plain flour, seasoned with salt and pepper
> 25g/1oz butter
> 2 onions, peeled and thinly sliced
> 2 lambs' kidneys, cored and sliced
> Salt and freshly ground black pepper
> 2 sprigs fresh rosemary, or half a teaspoonful dried rosemary
> 300-450ml/ ½ - ¾ pint stock, preferably lamb stock
> 225g/8oz medium-sized mushrooms, sliced
> 225g/8oz shortcrust pastry (made with 225g/8oz flour and
>     100g/4oz fat – if using ready-made pastry, you will need
>     340g/12oz)
> Milk or beaten egg to glaze

Pre-heat the oven to 180°C/350°F/Gas Mark 4. Coat the chops generously with the seasoned flour, heat the butter in a large frying pan and brown the chops on both sides. Arrange the chops in a pie dish and scatter the sliced onions on top. Add the sliced kidneys, season lightly and add the rosemary. Pour the stock into the frying pan and heat through, stirring to pick up all the residue of flour in the pan, and pour enough of the stock over the pie filling to just cover. Arrange the sliced mushrooms in overlapping layers to cover the filling. Roll out the pastry and cover the pie, sealing the edges well. Glaze with milk or beaten egg and cook in the pre-heated oven for about 40 minutes, or until the pastry is crisp.

In past times, Surrey was so famous as the county where chickens were fattened up for the London meat markets that its inhabitants were nicknamed 'Surrey Capons'. (A 'capon' is a cockerel that has been castrated, producing a bird with more tender meat.) A town particularly associated with fine fowl was Dorking, which was renowned for the famous Dorking Fowl, a breed of chicken that was once extensively bred there and was highly prized as both an egg layer and a table bird. There are three main colour variations: the Red, the Silver Grey and the Dark Dorking, and the cock has silver and green plumage. It is compact, plump in build and bred for the breast; it carries more meat in proportion to its size than any other fowl, and in quantity and flavour its flesh is excellent. As a layer, the hen compares favourably with any other birds of its size and weight. It was said to be a favourite with Queen Victoria, who would only eat eggs from the Dorking hen. A peculiar characteristic of the Dorking Fowl breed is that it possesses a fifth claw.

**DORKING, GREETINGS FROM DORKING POSTCARD c1935** D45069

# RECIPE

## CHICKEN BREASTS WITH A HONEY AND ORANGE GLAZE

'Well-fattened and tender, a fowl is to the cook what the canvas is to the painter; for do we not see it served boiled, roasted, fried, fricasseed, hashed, hot, cold, whole, dismembered, boned, broiled, stuffed, on dishes and in pies – always handy and ever acceptable?' Thus wrote Mrs Beeton in an enthusiastic ode to the chicken in the 1861 edition of her 'Book of Household Management'. Hopefully she would have approved of this recipe, which serves up chicken breasts with a honey and orange glaze. Locally produced honey made by busy Surrey bees can be found in many farm shops and local food stores around the county, and at the Crockford Bridge Farm Shop at Little Addlestone, near Weybridge, you can buy honey made by the bees right there on the farm. Serves 4-6.

> 4-6 chicken breasts, skin left on (this helps keep the meat
>   moist and juicy)
> Finely grated zest and juice of 2 oranges
> 3 tablespoonfuls honey
> Juice of half a lemon
> Salt and freshly ground pepper

Pre-heat the oven to 190°C/375°F/Gas Mark 5. Place the chicken breasts skin side down in a roasting tin or ovenproof dish. Mix the orange juice with the honey and 1 dessertspoonful of lemon juice, and season lightly with a little salt and pepper. Pour the liquid over the chicken and cover with a tightly-fitting piece of kitchen foil. Bake in the pre-heated oven for 20 minutes, then remove the foil and turn the chicken pieces over, to be skin side up. Return to the oven and cook for a further 20-30 minutes, depending on their size. To check if they are done, press one of the pieces with your finger – if it's still a bit soft, give it a bit longer. Serve with some of the honey and orange syrup spooned over each portion, which will have thickened by the time the chicken is cooked. Serve with some grated orange zest sprinkled over for decoration, if desired.

# RECIPE

## DEVILLED CHICKEN LEGS

'Devilling', or adding a mustard sauce to food, was very popular in Victorian and Edwardian times, and a recipe for Devilled Chicken Legs is given here. This hot, spicy dish could be eaten hot with strips of hot buttered toast, or taken on picnics or boating trips to be eaten cold. The photograph on the opposite page shows a party enjoying a day out on a steam launch at Molesey Lock on the River Thames in 1896, with the two maids surrounded by laden picnic baskets. A Victorian picnic meant more than a plate of cucumber sandwiches: Mrs Beeton decreed that no self-respecting picnicker should venture out without a hamper overflowing with joints of cold roast beef, fowls, parcels of duck, ham, tongue, veal pie, pigeon pie, lobster, and a collared calf's head, to be followed by stewed fruit, cabinet pudding, jam puffs and plum pie – all home-made, of course!

> 8 cooked chicken legs
> 2 teaspoonfuls English mustard powder
> 1 teaspoonful salt
> Half a teaspoonful freshly ground black pepper
> Half a teaspoonful cayenne pepper
> Half a teaspoonful paprika
> 2 teaspoonfuls mild curry powder
> 3 teaspoonfuls French mustard
> 50g/2oz butter
> 1 tablespoonful plain flour

Mix the mustard powder with half the salt, pepper, cayenne and paprika, the curry powder, and the French mustard and work to a paste, then blend in half the butter. Make 4 slits down the length of each chicken leg and spread a little of the devil mixture into each. Season the flour with the remaining salt, pepper, cayenne and paprika. Use to dust the chicken legs. Melt the remaining butter and brush over each leg. Place under a pre-heated hot grill and cook for 6 minutes, turning to brown the legs on all sides. Baste with the pan juices once or twice during cooking.

**EAST MOLESEY, STEAMBOAT IN THE LOCK
RIVER THAMES 1896** 38350x

# RECIPE

## CHIPSTEAD CHURDLES

Churdles are savoury snacks made in a triangular shape with the pastry edges folded up, like a three-sided tricorn hat, with the centre left open to show the savoury filling.

> 225g/8oz shortcrust pastry (made with 225g/8oz flour and 100g/4oz fat – if using ready-made pastry, you will need 340g/12oz)
> 1 tablespoonful browned breadcrumbs
> A small amount of grated cheese
> Bacon fat or vegetable oil for frying
> 1 large sliced onion
> 225g/8oz sliced lambs' liver
> 225g/8oz chopped bacon rashers or pieces, with the rind taken off
> 50g/2oz chopped mushrooms
> 1 medium cooking apple, peeled, cored and chopped
> 1 tablespoonful chopped parsley
> 1 teaspoonful dried rosemary
> Salt and pepper to taste
> Beaten egg, to glaze

Pre-heat the oven to 180°C/350°F/Gas Mark 4. Fry the onion, liver and bacon in the fat or oil until nicely browned. Mince or finely chop together the cooked onion, liver and bacon, then add the mushrooms, apple, parsley, rosemary and salt and pepper, and mix well. Roll out the pastry and cut out 15cm (6 inch) rounds. Brush some of the beaten egg around their edges and divide the filling mixture between the rounds. Fold up the edges of each pastry round to form a triangular shape and pinch the corners together to seal them, but leave the centre open to expose the filling. Mix together the breadcrumbs and cheese and sprinkle over the exposed centres. Place the Churdles on a baking sheet and brush with beaten egg. Bake in the pre-heated oven for about 30 minutes, until the pastry is golden. These are delicious served with redcurrant jelly.

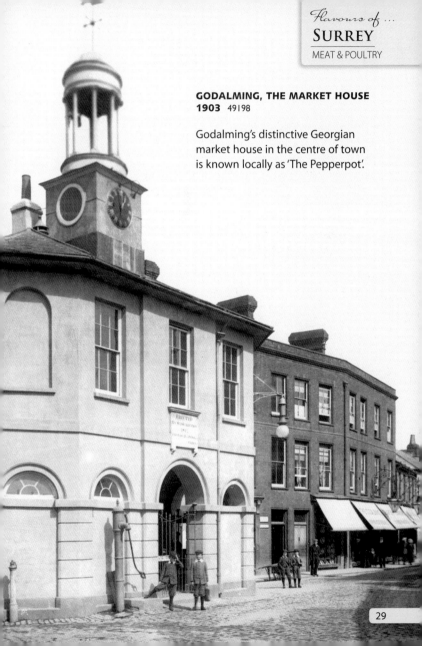

**GODALMING, THE MARKET HOUSE
1903** 49198

Godalming's distinctive Georgian
market house in the centre of town
is known locally as 'The Pepperpot'.

# RECIPE

### MYSTERIOUS PUDDING

This is a modernised version of another recipe collected from Surrey that was included in May Byron's cookery book 'Pot Luck' of 1914. It makes a very good steamed pudding with a soft, light texture. How did it get its intriguing name? That's the mystery!

> 2 medium eggs, separated
> 100g/4oz self-raising flour
> 100g/4oz butter, softened to room temperature
> 100g/4oz caster sugar
> 1 tablespoonful marmalade
> 2 tablespoonfuls milk

Butter the inside of a 1.2 litre (2 pint) pudding basin. Beat together the butter and sugar until creamy and fluffy. Gradually beat in the flour and then stir in the marmalade. Beat the eggs yolks and add them to the mixture with the milk, and mix it all together well. Whisk the eggs whites until the mixture is stiff and stands in peaks, then use a large metal spoon to fold them into the mixture, gently but thoroughly. Turn the mixture into the buttered pudding basin. Cover the top of the basin with its lid, or a piece of pleated greaseproof paper (to allow room for rising), and then a piece of pleated foil and tie down firmly with string. Place the basin in the top half of a steamer or stand it in a large saucepan filled with enough boiling water to come halfway up its side, cover the pan with its lid, and steam for about 1½ hours. Top up the pan with more boiling water from time to time if necessary, so it doesn't boil dry. When cooked, leave the pudding to stand in the basin for about 5 minutes before turning it out onto a warmed serving dish. Spread a little more marmalade on top, if desired. Serve hot, with custard, cream or perhaps the lemon sauce on page 33.

## SURREY

PUDDINGS & DESSERTS

Woking as we know it today grew up when the London to Southampton railway arrived in 1838, and is now one of Surrey's biggest towns. Woking has mushroomed in size and been redeveloped since it was first established in the 19th century, and few of the town's older Victorian buildings survive – the Old Bank on the corner of Chertsey Road and The Broadway, seen in this view, for instance, had no place in the modernised Woking of the second half of the 20th century.

**WOKING, THE OLD BANK 1901**  46342

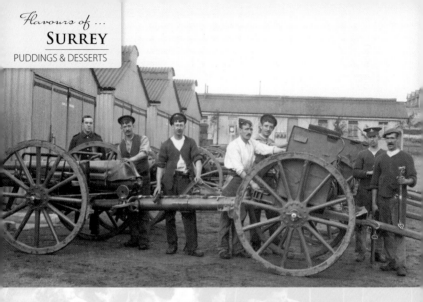

**DEEPCUT, GUNNERS AT WORK 1906** 55053

North-west Surrey is an upland region of sandy heaths and clumps of pines that in days gone by was unprofitable to the farmer and sparsely populated. Now much of the area is given over to the army, which moved into this part of the county in Victorian times. In the 1820s the Royal Military College's Senior Department was moved to the Sandhurst estate, just over the county boundary in Berkshire; it was later renamed the Military Staff College, and the settlement of Camberley grew up at its gates. This view shows a group of gunners from the Royal Field Artillery pausing in their task of servicing their heavy artillery outside the ordnance depot at Deepcut Camp near Camberley, which was built in 1901 and named after the long, deep cutting that was made in 1791-92 to carry the Basingstoke Canal across the high heathlands of west Surrey – completed in 1794, the canal linked the Wey and Godalming Navigation with Basingstoke. The recipe on the opposite page recalls Surrey's military connections, and is taken from the version Mrs Beeton included in the 1861 edition of her 'Book of Household Management'.

# RECIPE

## MILITARY PUDDINGS AND LEMON SAUCE

This should make 6 individual lemon-flavoured suet-and-breadcrumb puddings, to be served with a lemon sauce.

<u>For the puddings:</u>
175g/6oz shredded suet
175g/6oz soft white
   breadcrumbs
175g/6oz caster sugar
Grated zest and juice of
   1 lemon

<u>For the sauce:</u>
100g/4oz caster sugar
1 rounded tablespoonful
   cornflour
A pinch of salt
250ml/9 fl oz water
Finely grated zest and juice
   of 2 lemons
25g/1oz butter, cut into
   small pieces

Pre-heat the oven to 180°C/350°F/Gas Mark 4. Butter 6 individual ramekin pots or similar. Mix together the suet, breadcrumbs and sugar. Stir in the lemon zest and juice and mix well, breaking down any lumps to form a dry, crumbly mixture. Fill the prepared pots with the mixture, right up to the top as the puddings will sink down during cooking, but do not compact the mixture. Place the pots on a baking tray and bake in the pre-heated oven for 35-40 minutes, until the tops of the puddings are crisp and golden brown.

Make the lemon sauce whilst the puddings are cooking. Put the sugar, cornflour and salt in a saucepan and stir in the water a little at a time to make a smooth paste. Stir in the grated lemon zest and put the pan over a low heat. Cook gently, stirring all the time, until the mixture simmers and thickens. Continue simmering for about a minute then remove from the heat. Beat in the butter pieces one at a time to make a thick, glossy sauce, then stir in 3 tablespoonfuls of lemon juice. Keep the sauce warm until the puddings are ready.

When the puddings are cooked, leave them to stand for about 5 minutes. Then run the blade of a knife around the inside of the pots to loosen them, turn them out onto serving dishes and serve immediately, with lemon sauce poured over them.

**GODSTONE, CHURCH LANE 1905** 53284

In the 18th century, water that reputedly cured gout was being drawn from a well in Godstone that had been sunk beside a pear tree. No one could eat the fruit of the tree as it was so hard, but the Iron Peartree Water was much sought after, and could be bought at the White Hart Inn in the village for a shilling a bottle. People came from miles around to take the cure.

# RECIPE

## Spiced Pears

The early varieties of pears grown in country gardens in the past were often extremely hard, and many old recipes, like this, were devised for cooking them slowly until they softened. This is still a good way of using the hard cooking pears that are widely available in greengrocers and supermarkets and are relatively inexpensive. Ripe but firm dessert pears can also be prepared this way, but will only need a shorter cooking time. Serves 4.

    4 hard cooking pears (about 450g/1lb)
    75g/3oz caster sugar
    300ml/ ½ pint water
    Half a teaspoonful ground ginger
    1 small cinnamon stick
    2 whole cloves
    Finely grated rind and juice of 1 small lemon

Pre-heat the oven to 130°C/250°F/Gas Mark ½. Peel the pears, cut them in half lengthways and use a teaspoon or sharp knife to remove their cores. Lay the pear halves in a single layer in a flameproof casserole dish with a tight-fitting lid. Sprinkle them with the sugar, pour in the water and add the ginger, cinnamon stick, cloves, and the lemon rind and juice. Put the casserole dish over a medium heat and bring just up to simmering point, then cover the dish with its lid and place on a low shelf in the pre-heated oven. Cook for about 30 minutes, then turn the pear halves onto their other side and cook for a further 30 minutes, or until they are tender – very hard pears may need a longer cooking time. Remove the dish from the oven and either serve hot, or leave the pears to cool in the syrup and serve cold.

# RECIPE

### LORD JOHN RUSSELL'S PUDDING

This recipe was included by Florence White, founder of the English Folk Cookery Association, in her book 'Good Things in England' of 1932, in which she states 'this recipe for a very delicious iced pudding is from Rusley Lodge, Esher, 1863'. This version has been adapted to make a smaller pudding than in her recipe, and with glycerine substituted for the setting ingredient instead of isinglass. Modern cooks will also need to set the pudding in their freezer, since few of us nowadays can do as directed in the original version and put the pudding 'into an ice-cave' in the grounds of our own humble homes! Serves 4-6.

3 egg yolks
450ml/ ¾ pint whole (full fat) milk
25g/1oz caster sugar
Finely grated zest of 1 small lemon
5 leaves of gelatine
300ml/ ½ pint double cream
1 tablespoonful brandy
2-3 drops almond essence
1 tablespoonful chopped mixed candied peel
1 tablespoonful glacé cherries, cut into quarters
1 tablespoonful dried or crystallised pineapple,
  cut into very small pieces

Whisk the milk and egg yolks together in a basin, then stir in the sugar and lemon zest. Set the basin over a pan of simmering water (but not boiling) and stir continually until the custard thickens enough to coat the spoon. Remove from the heat and keep stirring as it continues to cook and thicken in the pan, then leave to cool down for a few minutes. Soak the gelatine leaves in water as

36

instructed on the packet, then squeeze out any excess moisture and stir them into the custard mixture until dissolved. Stir in the cream, brandy, almond essence and all the fruit, and mix it all together well. Pour the mixture into a freezer-proof container, cover with its lid and place in the freezer for 2 hours. Remove and beat the mixture well with a wooden spoon to break up the crystals of ice that are forming around the edges, and stir them through the mixture. Cover again and return to the freezer for another 3-4 hours, until the mixture is firm and creamy. Serve accompanied with fan wafers, sponge fingers or sweet crisp biscuits.

**FRIMLEY GREEN, AN OLD COTTAGE 1906** 54907

# RECIPE

### SURREY SYLLABUB

In the 1530s, Henry VIII built a palace on the Oatlands estate near Weybridge; that Tudor palace was demolished after the Civil War of the 17th century, and the Oatlands Park Hotel now stands on its site. Syllabub was a very popular dessert in Tudor times, and just the sort of dish that would have been enjoyed at Oatlands in the past. It still makes a delicious dessert, made with cream and either white wine or, as in this old recipe collected in Surrey, sherry and brandy. Serves 6 – you only need to serve syllabub in small helpings, as it is very rich.

> 300ml/ ½ pint double cream
> 50g/2oz caster sugar
> Finely grated zest and juice of 1 unwaxed lemon
> 60ml/4 tablespoonfuls medium dry sherry
> 1 tablespoonful brandy
> A little freshly grated nutmeg (optional)
> A few thin strips of lemon peel, to decorate

Put the lemon zest and juice into a large bowl, add the sherry, brandy and sugar, and stir until the sugar has completely dissolved. Stir in the cream, and a little freshly grated nutmeg, if using. Whip the mixture until it goes thick and soft peaks form. Spoon the mixture into wine glasses or small glass sundae dishes and chill until ready to serve, decorated with a few thin strips of lemon peel. Syllabub is nice served with sponge fingers or sweet crisp biscuits.

BURCE & C°°

**ADDLESTONE, CHILDREN OUTSIDE THE HOLLY TREE INN 1904** 51701x

**GREAT BOOKHAM, POLESDEN LACEY 1929** 82423

The popularity of Surrey as an ideal area for a country retreat, from the 15th and 16th centuries onwards, helped to encourage and develop the county's food production. In the Tudor period, the great palaces of Hampton Court, Nonsuch, Oatlands and Richmond created an almost insatiable demand for produce when the court was in residence, and this was increased as the rich and aristocracy built their great houses in the county. The great landowners became interested in their kitchen gardens as well as their parks and pleasure gardens, eagerly comparing notes about new seeds and varieties of plants. Hot houses became fashionable, and exotic items like peaches, nectarines and apricots were grown. The first person in England to have grown oranges in his garden is believed to have been Sir Francis Carew in the 1560s at his estate at Beddington near Croydon, which was in Surrey in his day, although the fruit would not have been up to much in the English climate. Many of those great country houses are now in the care of the National Trust and open to the public, including Polesden Lacey on the southern edge of Great Bookham, north-west of Dorking.

# RECIPE

## ORANGE MOUSSE

Polesden Lacy was the home of the famous society hostess Mrs Margaret Greville from 1906 until her death in 1942, when she left the property to the National Trust. Her collection of fine paintings, furniture, porcelain and silver is displayed in the reception room and galleries, as it was at the time of her lavish house parties. Her guests included royalty, the rich and famous, literary figures and prominent politicians, one of whom was the Labour politician and former Prime Minister Ramsay Macdonald (1866-1937), who was a visitor there in October 1936; the menu book records that he was served salade nicoise and orange mousse. The orange mousse that Mrs Greville's celebrated chef created was probably a much more elaborate affair than the version given here, but this makes a delicious light, creamy dessert. Serves 6-8.

Finely grated zest and juice of 3 oranges
250g/9oz soft white cheese, like Philadelphia or equivalent
125g/5oz caster sugar
200ml/7fl oz double cream
3 egg whites

Put the soft cheese into a bowl with the orange zest and 50g (2oz) of the sugar, and beat until soft and well combined. Whisk the egg whites until stiff and soft peaks form. Keep whisking as you gradually add in the remaining sugar, until you have a smooth, glossy mixture. Use a large metal spoon to fold it lightly into the soft cheese mixture. Add enough of the orange juice to the cream to make it up to 300ml (10fl oz), whip the mixture until soft peaks form, and fold this lightly but thoroughly into the mousse mixture. Spoon the mixture into a pretty serving dish, or 6-8 individual pots or glass sundae dishes if preferred. Chill in the refrigerator for at least 2 hours, or until just before ready to serve – this can be made in advance and left to chill overnight if necessary.

**LEATHERHEAD, CHURCH STREET 1913** 66111

# RECIPE

## DOUGH CAKES

The key ingredient of these cakes is lard, the fat that was rendered down when a pig was killed, hence their other name of Lardie Cakes. Lard was the most widely available cooking fat to housewives and bakers in the past and was often used in baking instead of butter, which was, and still is, much more expensive, but butter can be used in this recipe if preferred. These cakes are made from yeasted bread dough that is rolled and folded several times over layers of lard, sugar and currants, and they were often made on baking day, using up any leftover bread dough to make a tasty treat.

<u>For the dough:</u>
450g/1lb plain flour
1 teaspoonful salt
25g/1oz lard or butter
1 x 7g sachet (2 rounded teaspoonfuls) easy-bake dried yeast
1 teaspoonful caster sugar
300ml/10fl oz warm water

<u>For the filling:</u>
50g/2oz lard or butter, well softened
50g/2oz caster sugar
Half a teaspoonful ground mixed spice
50g/2oz currants
A little milk to finish

To make the dough: Mix the flour and salt and rub in the 25g (1oz) lard or butter. Stir in the dried yeast and sugar, and then the warm water. Mix it all together well, then turn out on to a floured surface and knead. Cover the dough with a cloth and leave in a warm place until it has doubled in size, then knead again.

**MERROW, THE FORGE 1913** 65231

Roll out the dough into a rectangle about 5mm (¼ in) thick. Spread the dough with one third of the softened lard or butter. Mix the 50g (2oz) sugar and mixed spice, and sprinkle one third of the mixture over the rolled-out dough. Fold the dough into three, half turn it and press the edges together. Roll out the dough again, and repeat the process twice more, but sprinkle the currants over the last sugar and spice mixture. Roll out to about 2cm (¾ in) thick and cut into rounds of 7-10cm (3-4 in) diameter. Decorate the surfaces by scoring across them a couple of times with a sharp knife and place the rounds on a greased baking sheet. Cover again with a cloth and leave to rise in a warm place for another 30 minutes. Pre-heat the oven to 200°C/400°F/Gas Mark 6 and bake for 15-20 minutes, until the cakes are risen and golden but not over-browned. Take out of the oven and brush the tops of the cakes with a little milk whilst they are hot, to give them a light glaze. These are best eaten the same day they are made, especially whilst still warm from the oven.

# RECIPE

### SPICE CAKE

This recipe makes a good, simple fruit cake that needs no eggs, so could be made at the time of year when the hens weren't laying, or whenever eggs were scarce.

> 450g/1lb plain flour
> 4 teaspoonfuls mixed spice
> A pinch of salt
> 225g/8oz Trex or similar baking fat, softened
> 175g/6oz caster sugar
> 175g/6oz sultanas
> 175g/6oz currants
> 300ml/ ½ pint milk
> 2 teaspoonfuls white wine vinegar
> 2 teaspoonfuls bicarbonate of soda
> 2 tablespoonfuls demerara or soft brown sugar,
>   to finish

Pre-heat the oven to 160°C/325°F/Gas Mark 3. Grease and line a 20cm (8in) square cake tin.

Sift the flour, spice and salt into a mixing bowl and rub in the fat. Add the caster sugar and dried fruit and mix well. Blend the bicarbonate of soda to a smooth paste with a little of the milk, then mix it with the rest of the milk and the vinegar and stir the liquid into the mixture. Mix well to form a smooth dough, and turn it into the prepared tin. Smooth the top, and sprinkle with the demerara or soft brown sugar. Bake for 1-1¼ hours or a little longer if necessary, until a skewer comes out clean. Remove from the oven and leave the cake to cool in the tin before turning out.

**GUILDFORD, HIGH STREET
1910** 63060

PEAK
&
LUNN

# RECIPE

## CLAREMONT GINGERBREAD

Claremont is an 18th-century Palladian mansion near Esher, which was originally built in the 1770s for Lord Clive of India. In the 19th century it was the home of Queen Victoria's son and daughter-in-law, the Duke and Duchess of Albany. The house at Claremont is now used as a school, but the grounds are owned and managed by the National Trust and are open to the public. This recipe makes a very nice light, soft gingerbread.

> 225g/8oz plain flour
> 1 teaspoonful bicarbonate of soda
> 1 teaspoonful ground ginger
> 1 heaped teaspoonful ground rice (look for this near the pudding rice on supermarket shelves)
> 100g/4oz butter or margarine
> 100g/4oz soft brown sugar, light or dark as you prefer
> 1 tablespoonful black treacle
> 1 egg, beaten
> 2 tablespoonfuls milk

Pre-heat the oven to 180°C/350°F/Gas Mark 4. Grease a baking tin about 20cm (8in) square.

Sift together the flour, bicarbonate of soda and ginger. Stir in the ground rice. Put the butter, sugar and treacle in a saucepan and heat gently over a low heat, stirring, until the butter has melted and the sugar has dissolved. Remove the pan from the heat and stir the liquid into the flour mixture. Mix together well, then stir in the milk to form a smooth batter, and last of all stir in the beaten egg. Turn the mixture into the prepared baking tin and bake in the pre-heated oven for 25-30 minutes, until the top is risen and firm to the touch but before the edges start to brown and burn. Leave the gingerbread to cool in the tin before cutting it into squares, then store in an airtight container. This is best left for at least a day before eating.

**BOX HILL, ON BANK HOLIDAY 1906** 55711av

Since the early 19th century, when road and train systems improved, visitors have flocked to Surrey to visit its famous beauty spots like the valley of the Devil's Punchbowl, near Hindhead, and Box Hill, near Dorking. The popularity of Box Hill reached an apogee during the late Victorian and Edwardian era, when the railway and the advent of the bicycle brought it within easy reach of day-trippers from London. Box Hill also features in Jane Austen's novel 'Emma' of 1815, which is set in Surrey, when some of the characters go there to enjoy a day out and what becomes an eventful picnic. They are most enthusiastic when they reach their destination: 'Seven miles were travelled in expectation of enjoyment and everyone had a burst of admiration on arriving.'

# RECIPE

## PICNIC CAKE

The mixture of spices and honey in this cake gives it a lovely flavour. It has quite a dense texture that keeps together well, which makes it ideal to take on a picnic or include in a lunch box.

> 100g/4oz butter or margarine, softened to room temperature
> 225g/8oz caster sugar or soft brown sugar
> 3 eggs, beaten
> 175g/6oz self-raising flour
> ¼ teaspoonful salt
> ½ teaspoonful ground nutmeg
> ½ teaspoonful ground cinnamon
> 2 tablespoonfuls milk
> 2 tablespoonfuls runny honey
> ¼ teaspoonful bicarbonate of soda
> 175g/6oz raisins or sultanas
> 175g/6oz chopped walnuts
> 6-8 walnut halves, to decorate

Pre-heat the oven to 160°C/325°F/Gas Mark 3. Grease and line a 900g (2 lb) loaf tin.

Sift the flour, salt and spices together into a bowl. In a separate bowl, cream together the butter or margarine and sugar until light and fluffy. Beat in a little of the beaten eggs and then some of the flour mixture. Repeat alternately until all is used up. Warm the milk very slightly in a pan, add the honey, then sprinkle in the bicarbonate of soda, stir until dissolved and add to the cake mixture. Add the chopped walnuts and dried fruit, and combine it all together well. Turn the mixture into the cake tin and bake just below the centre of the pre-heated oven for 1-1¼ hours, then lightly press the walnut halves into the top of the cake and bake for a further 40-45 minutes. Cover the top of the cake with kitchen foil if it seems to be browning too quickly. Leave the cake to cool in the tin before turning out on a wire rack and leaving to cool completely. Serve cut into slices.

## HINDHEAD, A CHARABANC AND THE POST OFFICE 1906  55506x

# FRANCIS FRITH

## PIONEER   VICTORIAN   PHOTOGRAPHER

Francis Frith, founder of the world-famous photographic archive, was a complex and multi-talented man. A devout Quaker and a highly successful Victorian businessman, he was philosophical by nature and pioneering in outlook. By 1855 he had already established a wholesale grocery business in Liverpool, and sold it for the astonishing sum of £200,000, which is the equivalent today of over £15,000,000. Now in his thirties, and captivated by the new science of photography, Frith set out on a series of pioneering journeys up the Nile and to the Near East.

## INTRIGUE AND EXPLORATION

He was the first photographer to venture beyond the sixth cataract of the Nile. Africa was still the mysterious 'Dark Continent', and Stanley and Livingstone's historic meeting was a decade into the future. The conditions for picture taking confound belief. He laboured for hours in his wicker dark-room in the sweltering heat of the desert, while the volatile chemicals fizzed dangerously in their trays. Back in London he exhibited his photographs and was 'rapturously cheered' by members of the Royal Society. His reputation as a photographer was made overnight.

## VENTURE OF A LIFE-TIME

By the 1870s the railways had threaded their way across the country, and Bank Holidays and half-day Saturdays had been made obligatory by Act of Parliament. All of a sudden the working man and his family were able to enjoy days out, take holidays, and see a little more of the world.

With typical business acumen, Francis Frith foresaw that these new tourists would enjoy having souvenirs to commemorate their days out. For the next thirty years he travelled the country by train and by pony and trap, producing fine photographs of seaside resorts and beauty spots that were keenly bought by millions of Victorians. These prints were painstakingly pasted into family albums and pored over during the dark nights of winter, rekindling precious memories of summer excursions. Frith's studio was soon supplying retail shops all over the country, and by 1890 F Frith & Co had become the greatest specialist photographic publishing company in the world, with over 2,000 sales outlets, and pioneered the picture postcard.

## FRANCIS FRITH'S LEGACY

Francis Frith had died in 1898 at his villa in Cannes, his great project still growing. By 1970 the archive he created contained over a third of a million pictures showing 7,000 British towns and villages.

Frith's legacy to us today is of immense significance and value, for the magnificent archive of evocative photographs he created provides a unique record of change in the cities, towns and villages throughout Britain over a century and more. Frith and his fellow studio photographers revisited locations many times down the years to update their views, compiling for us an enthralling and colourful pageant of British life and character.

We are fortunate that Frith was dedicated to recording the minutiae of everyday life. For it is this sheer wealth of visual data, the painstaking chronicle of changes in dress, transport, street layouts, buildings, housing and landscape that captivates us so much today, offering us a powerful link with the past and with the lives of our ancestors.

Computers have now made it possible for Frith's many thousands of images to be accessed almost instantly. The archive offers every one of us an opportunity to examine the places where we and our families have lived and worked down the years. Its images, depicting our shared past, are now bringing pleasure and enlightenment to millions around the world a century and more after his death.

For further information visit: www.francisfrith.com

## INTERIOR DECORATION

Frith's photographs can be seen framed and as giant wall murals in thousands of pubs, restaurants, hotels, banks, retail stores and other public buildings throughout Britain. These provide interesting and attractive décor, generating strong local interest and acting as a powerful reminder of gentler days in our increasingly busy and frenetic world.

## FRITH PRODUCTS

All Frith photographs are available as prints and posters in a variety of different sizes and styles. In the UK we also offer a range of other gift and stationery products illustrated with Frith photographs, although many of these are not available for delivery outside the UK – see our web site for more information on the products available for delivery in your country.

## THE INTERNET

Over 100,000 photographs of Britain can be viewed and purchased on the Frith web site. The web site also includes memories and reminiscences contributed by our customers, who have personal knowledge of localities and of the people and properties depicted in Frith photographs. If you wish to learn more about a specific town or village you may find these reminiscences fascinating to browse. Why not add your own comments if you think they would be of interest to others? See **www.francisfrith.com**

## PLEASE HELP US BRING FRITH'S PHOTOGRAPHS TO LIFE

Our authors do their best to recount the history of the places they write about. They give insights into how particular towns and villages developed, they describe the architecture of streets and buildings, and they discuss the lives of famous people who lived there. But however knowledgeable our authors are, the story they tell is necessarily incomplete.

Frith's photographs are so much more than plain historical documents. They are living proofs of the flow of human life down the generations. They show real people at real moments in history; and each of those people is the son or daughter of someone, the brother or sister, aunt or uncle, grandfather or grandmother of someone else. All of them lived, worked and played in the streets depicted in Frith's photographs.

We would be grateful if you would give us your insights into the places shown in our photographs: the streets and buildings, the shops, businesses and industries. Post your memories of life in those streets on the Frith website: what it was like growing up there, who ran the local shop and what shopping was like years ago; if your workplace is shown tell us about your working day and what the building is used for now. Read other visitors' memories and reconnect with your shared local history and heritage. With your help more and more Frith photographs can be brought to life, and vital memories preserved for posterity, and for the benefit of historians in the future.

Wherever possible, we will try to include some of your comments in future editions of our books. Moreover, if you spot errors in dates, titles or other facts, please let us know, because our archive records are not always completely accurate—they rely on 140 years of human endeavour and hand-compiled records. You can email us using the contact form on the website.

Thank you!

For further information, trade, or author enquiries
please contact us at the address below:

**The Francis Frith Collection, 6 Oakley Business Park,
Wylye Road, Dinton, Wiltshire SP3 5EU England.**
Tel: +44 (0)1722 716 376  Fax: +44 (0)1722 716 881
e-mail: sales@francisfrith.co.uk  **www.francisfrith.com**